AF573843

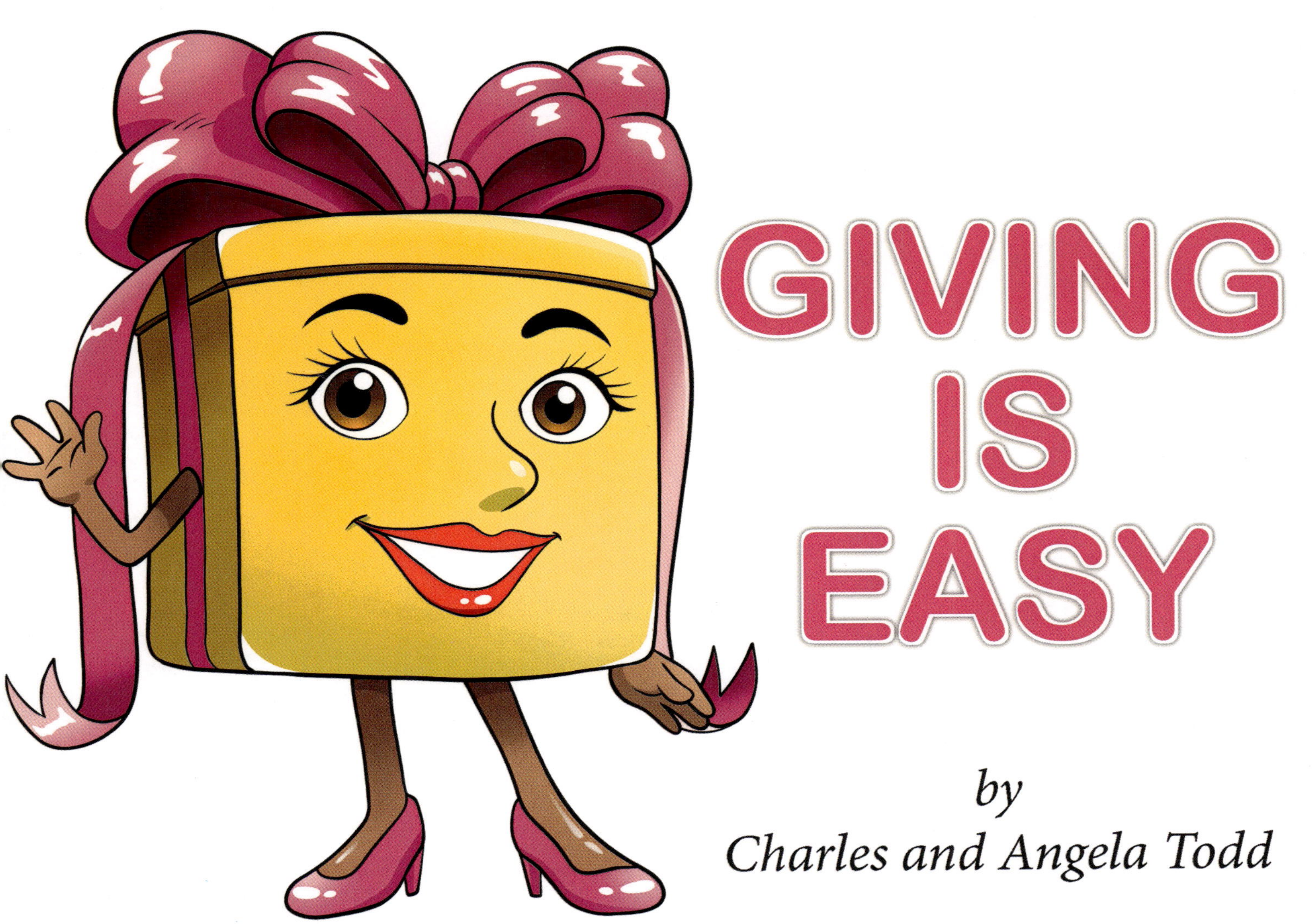

GIVING IS EASY

by

Charles and Angela Todd

GIVING IS EASY

BEST-SELLING AUTHOR, CHARLES TODD
BEST-SELLING AUTHOR, ANGELA TODD
ILLUSTRATOR, FUAD SY

FOR MORE INFORMATION CONTACT PUBLISHER:
TODD WORLDWIDE MINISTRIES 981 HIGHWAY 98E, STE 3-111, DESTIN, FL 32541
WWW.MONEYMIKEANDTHEGANG.COM

PAPERBACK # - ISBN: 978-1-953398-08-6
HARDCOVER # - ISBN: 978-1-953398-06-2
ELECTRONIC # - ISBN: 978-1-953398-07-9

FOREWORD

Giving is as easy as blowing a kiss!

To the parents who selected the second book from the Money Mike and The Gang™ series, Giving Is Easy, starring Giving Grace, to read to their children, we salute you! The message of giving is another supernatural principle that governs increase, promotion, and biblical success. As mentioned in the first Money Mike book Foreword, Money Is Easy, most people wait to take money seriously and only begin thinking about giving and investing later in their adult lives. Then, once they get in the game, they try so hard to play catch-up that they never reach their ultimate goals for success. The solution to breaking late patterns of defeat is putting Biblical increase secrets into action early. Most importantly, breaking every misconception in the mind that *I don't have enough money to give.*

Putting giving into action has proven successful for our family. We'd like to open up your mind to a simple principle; giving into the Kingdom of God to advance the gospel causes a multiplication factor back to you. Quite different from the world's system of when you give, you are depleted. There are so many wonderful scriptures that back up giving. One most Christians know is Malachi 3:10, "Bring the whole tithe into the storehouse, that there may be food in my house. Test me in this," says the Lord Almighty, "and see if I will not throw open the floodgates of Heaven and pour out so much blessing that there will not be room enough to store it." This is the only time in the Bible God says to test him. Some other translations say prove. Think about that, *selah.* If the Lord Almighty challenges me with my giving, you can bet your bottom dollar I'm going to prove it! And if you think tithing is not for us today and under the Old Testament, then we encourage you to study Genesis 14:18 and Hebrews 7; Abraham tithing to Melchizedek (with no lineage) before the law was given, which honors the seed, proclaiming the life of Christ. *Selah.*

In closing, as a general observation, children don't have to be taught to be selfish. We've all dealt with "Mine!" It's a trait that good parents correct. As parents and authors, it is our hope and heart that the Money Mike & The Gang™ characters will also aid in this correction and plant seeds early in childhood development to teach kids and parents how to leave an inheritance for their children's children for future generations to follow.

TITHE
SAVE
INVEST
GIVE
MUAH!
Giving Grace
Saving Sam
Loan Shark
LOAN SHARK
Money Mike

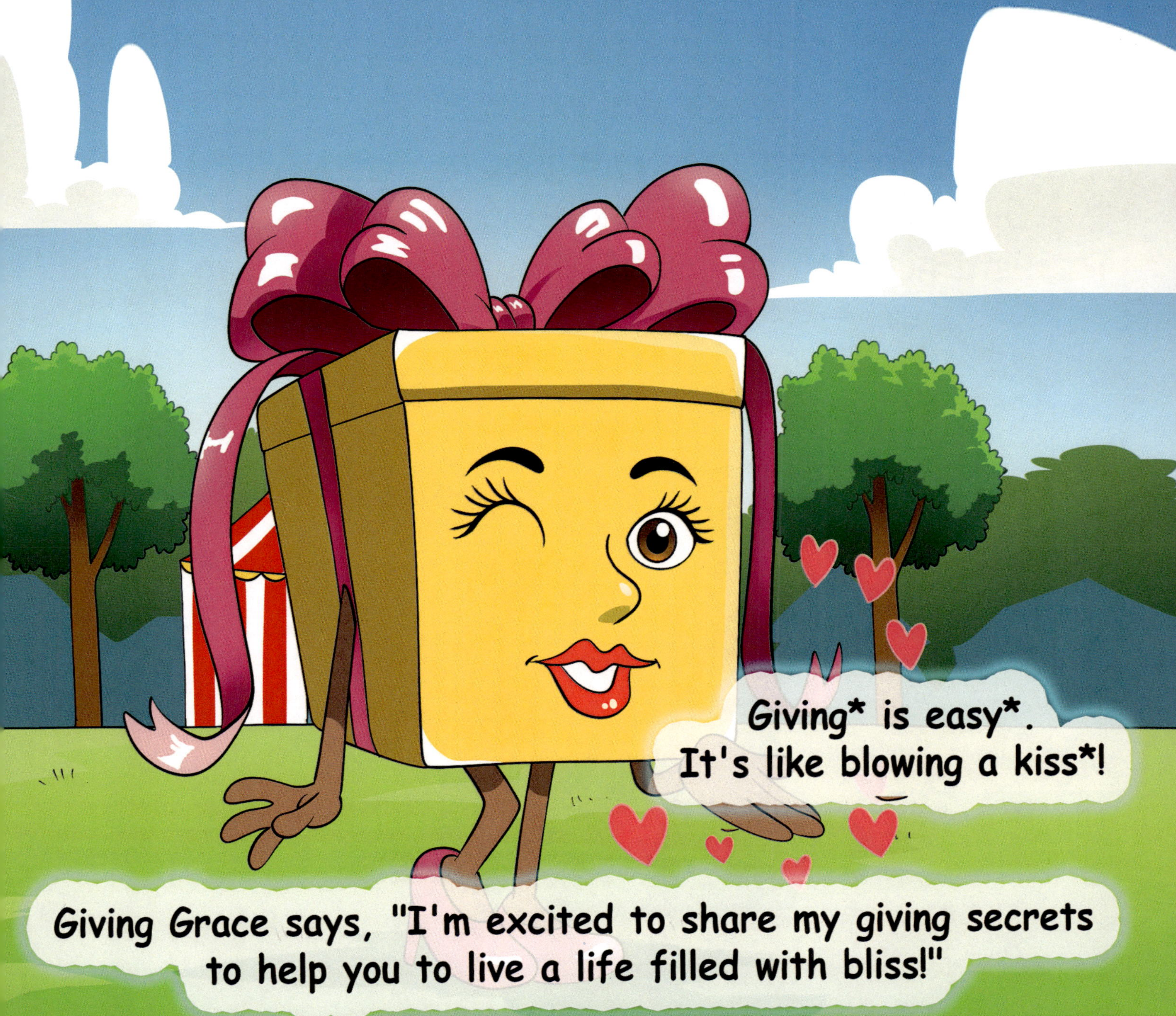

*Glossary of Terms with Scripture References (in alphabetical order) pages 26/27/28

When God blesses* you
with a family, a job, or friends,
Giving Grace says, "Find ways to say 'thank you.'
This is a humble* response* that pleases* God to no end."

*Glossary of Terms with Scripture References (in alphabetical order) pages 25/28/29/30

Giving to people will bless you back.
Giving Grace says, "It's like a boomerang* you throw; God will return what you give and make sure you won't lack*."

*Glossary of Terms with Scripture References (in alphabetical order) pages 26/29

*Glossary of Terms with Scripture References (in alphabetical order) pages 27/28

*Glossary of Terms with Scripture References (in alphabetical order) pages 26/28/29

*Glossary of Terms with Scripture References (in alphabetical order) page 25

*Glossary of Terms with Scripture References (in alphabetical order) page 31

*Glossary of Terms with Scripture References (in alphabetical order) page 30

*Glossary of Terms with Scripture References (in alphabetical order) page 29

Because that's who God* is from Heaven above.

*Glossary of Terms with Scripture References (in alphabetical order) page 27

Money Mike says, "It's good to plan* carefully
and give with a purpose*.
This allows God to bless you with an overflowing surplus*."

*Glossary of Terms with Scripture References (in alphabetical order) pages 29/30/31

*Glossary of Terms with Scripture References (in alphabetical order) pages 25/29/30/31

*Glossary of Terms with Scripture References (in alphabetical order) pages 25/26

Money Mike says, "When you tithe, God will protect* your money from the bad guys, and even from unexpected* things that may arise."

*Glossary of Terms with Scripture References (in alphabetical order) pages 29/30/31

*Glossary of Terms with Scripture References (in alphabetical order) pages 26/27

Money Mike and Giving Grace both agree,
"When you prayerfully* give to those in need,
God will continue to give you much more seed."

*Glossary of Terms with Scripture References (in alphabetical order) page 29

*Glossary of Terms with Scripture References (in alphabetical order) pages 27/28

*Glossary of Terms with Scripture References (in alphabetical order) page 30

*Glossary of Terms with Scripture References (in alphabetical order) page 25

*Glossary of Terms with Scripture References (in alphabetical order) page 27

*Glossary of Terms with Scripture References (in alphabetical order) page 31

*Glossary of Terms with Scripture References (in alphabetical order) page 31

INVEST
SAVE
Money Mike and Giving Grace both blow a kiss,
"Now go tell a friend about how giving is easy
so they too can live in bliss*!"

*GLOSSARY OF TERMS WITH SCRIPTURE REFERENCES (IN ALPHABETICAL ORDER)

Accept (v)—To take or receive (something offered); receive with approval or favor.

Psalm 6:9 (NIV)—The Lord has heard my cry for mercy; the Lord accepts my prayer.

Altar (n)—An elevated place or structure, as a mound or platform at which religious rites are performed.

Genesis 13:4 (ICB)—It was the place where Abram had built an altar before. So he worshiped the Lord there.

Applaud (v)—To clap the hands as an expression of approval, appreciation, acclamation, etc.

Psalm 117 (MSG)—Praise God, everybody! Applaud God, all people! His love has taken over our lives; God's faithful ways are eternal. Hallelujah!

Ask (v)(2)—To request information about.

Matthew 7:7 (NIV)—Ask and it will be given to you; seek and you will find; knock and the door will be opened to you.

Blesses (to bless, blessed, blessing) (v)(3)—To bestow good of any kind upon.

Deuteronomy 15:6 (AMP)—When the Lord your God blesses you as He has promised you, then you will lend to many nations, but you will not borrow; and you will rule over many nations, but they will not rule over you.

Bliss (n)—Supreme happiness; utter joy or contentment.

Proverbs 29:18 (TPT)—When there is no clear prophetic vision, people quickly wander astray. But when you follow the revelation of the Word, heaven's bliss fills your soul.

Blood (n)—The fluid that circulates in the principal vascular system of human beings and other vertebrates in humans consisting of plasma in which the red blood cells, white blood cells, and platelets are suspended.

1 John 1:7 (KJV)—But if we walk in the light, as he is in the light, we have fellowship one with another, and the blood of Jesus Christ his Son cleanseth us from all sin.

Boomerang (v)(4)—To come back or return, as a boomerang.

Luke 6:37 (MSG)—Don't pick on people, jump on their failures, criticize their faults—unless, of course, you want the same treatment. Don't condemn those who are down; that hardness can boomerang. Be easy on people; you'll find life a lot easier.

Church (n)—A building for public Christian worship.

Matthew 16:18 (MSG)—Jesus came back, "God bless you, Simon, son of Jonah! You didn't get that answer out of books or from teachers. My Father in heaven, God himself, let you in on this secret of who I really am. And now I'm going to tell you who you are, really are. You are Peter, a rock. This is the rock on which I will put together my church, a church so expansive with energy that not even the gates of hell will be able to keep it out.

Donation (n)—An act or instance of presenting something as a gift, grant, or contribution.

2 Corinthians 9:8 (AMPC)—And God is able to make all grace (every favor and earthly blessing) come to you in abundance, so that you may always and under all circumstances and whatever the need be self-sufficient [possessing enough to require no aid or support and furnished in abundance for every good work and charitable donation].

Easy (adj)—Not hard or difficult; requiring no great labor or effort.

Matthew 11:30 (WE)—What I tell you to do is easy. What I give you to carry is not heavy.

Expect (v)—To look forward to; regard as likely to happen; anticipate the occurrence or the coming of.

Proverbs 11:23 (NLT)—The godly can look forward to a reward, while the wicked can expect only judgment.

Express (v)—To put (thought) into words; utter or state.

Job 33:3 (AMP)—My words will express the uprightness of my heart, And my lips will speak what they know with utter sincerity.

Favored (adj)—Regarded or treated with preference or partiality.

Psalm 1:1 (AMP)—Blessed [fortunate, prosperous, and favored by God] is the man who does not walk in the counsel of the wicked [following their advice and example], Nor stand in the path of sinners, Nor sit [down to rest] in the seat of scoffers (ridiculers).

Giving (to give, v)—To present voluntarily and without expecting compensation; bestow.

Luke 6:38 (DLNT)—Be giving, and it will be given to you. They will give a good measure— having been pressed down, having been shaken, running over— into your fold [of the garment]. For with what measure you measure, it will be measured-back to you.

God (n)(4)—A nebulous powerful force imagined to be responsible for one's fate.

Deuteronomy 8:18 (NIV)—But remember the Lord your God, for it is he who gives you the ability to produce wealth, and so confirms his covenant, which he swore to your ancestors, as it is today.

Good (adj)—Morally excellent; virtuous; righteous; pious.

Psalm 107:1 (AMP)—O give thanks to the Lord, for He is good; For His compassion and lovingkindness endure forever!

Grace (n)—A manifestation of favor, especially by a superior.

John 1:17 (NIV)—For the law was given through Moses; grace and truth came through Jesus Christ.

Happy (adj)—Delighted, pleased, or glad, as over a particular thing.

Proverbs 3:13 (KJV)—Happy is the man that findeth wisdom, and the man that getteth understanding.

Harvest (v)(8)—To gain, win, or use (a prize, product, or result of any past act, process, etc.).

Matthew 9:38 (KJV)—Pray ye therefore the Lord of the harvest, that he will send forth labourers into his harvest.

Heart (n)(3)—The center of the total personality, especially with reference to intuition, feeling, or emotion.

Matthew 5:8 (NIV)—Blessed are the pure in heart, for they will see God.

Heaven (n)—The abode of God, the angels, and the spirits of the righteous after death; the place or state of existence of the blessed after the mortal life.

Psalm 14:2 (KJV)—The Lord looked down from heaven upon the children of men, to see if there were any that did understand, and seek God.

Humble (adj)—Not proud or arrogant; modest.

James 4:10 (NIV)—Humble yourselves before the Lord, and he will lift you up.

Joy (n)—The emotion of great delight or happiness caused by something exceptionally good or satisfying; keen pleasure; elation.

Psalm 35:27 (BRG)—Let them shout for joy, and be glad, that favour my righteous cause: yea, let them say continually, Let the Lord be magnified, which hath pleasure in the prosperity of his servant.

Key (n)(4)—Something that affords a means of access.

Matthew 16:19 (NKJV)—And I will give you the keys of the kingdom of heaven, and whatever you bind on earth will be bound in heaven, and whatever you loose on earth will be loosed in heaven.

Kiss (v)—To touch or press with the lips slightly pursed, and then often to part them and to emit a smacking sound, in an expression of affection, love, greeting, reverence, etc.

1 Peter 5:14 (AMPC) - Salute one another with a kiss of love [the symbol of mutual affection]. To all of you that are in Christ Jesus (the Messiah), may there be peace (every kind of peace and blessing, especially peace with God, and freedom from fears, agitating passions, and moral conflicts). Amen (so be it).

Lack (n)—Deficiency or absence of something needed, desirable, or customary.

Psalm 34:10 (TPT)—Even the strong and the wealthy grow weak and hungry, but those who passionately pursue the Lord will never lack any good thing.

Love (v)—A profoundly tender, passionate affection for another person.

1 John 4:8 (NIV)—Whoever does not love does not know God, because God is love.

Money (n)—Any circulating medium of exchange, including coins, paper money, and demand deposits.

Proverbs 13:11 (NIV)—Dishonest money dwindles away, but whoever gathers money little by little makes it grow.

Need (n)(2)—A lack of something wanted or deemed necessary.

Psalm 23:1 (NLT)—The Lord is my shepherd; I have all that I need.

Part (n)(2)—An essential or integral attribute or quality.

Psalm 101:3 (CEV)—I refuse to be corrupt or to take part in anything crooked, essential or integral attribute or quality.

Plan (n)(3)—A specific project or definite purpose.

Psalm 20:4 (CEB)—Let God grant what is in your heart and fulfill all your plans.

Pleases (v) please—To act to the pleasure or satisfaction of.

Proverbs 16:7 (AMPC)—When a man's ways please the Lord, He makes even his enemies to be at peace with him.

Prayerfully (adj)—Given to, characterized by, or expressive of prayer; devout.

Psalm 119:148 (MSG)—I stayed awake all night, prayerfully pondering your promise.

Principle (n)—An accepted or professed rule of action or conduct.

Psalm 111:10 (NET)—To obey the Lord is the fundamental principle for wise living; all who carry out his precepts acquire good moral insight. He will receive praise forever.

Produce (v)(11)—To create economic value; bring crops, goods, etc. to a point at which they will command a price.

Genesis 1:11 (NIV)—Then God said, "Let the land produce vegetation: seed-bearing plants and trees on the land that bear fruit with seed in it, according to their various kinds." And it was so.

Protect (v)—To defend or guard from attack, invasion, loss, annoyance, insult, etc.; cover or shield from injury or danger.

Deuteronomy 23:14 (NIV)—For the Lord your God moves about in your camp to protect you and to deliver your enemies to you. Your camp must be holy, so that he will not see among you anything indecent and turn away from you.

Purpose (n)(2)—An intended or desired result; end; aim; goal.

2 Corinthians 9:7 (AMP)—Let each one give [thoughtfully and with purpose] just as he has decided in his heart, not grudgingly or under compulsion, for God loves a cheerful giver [and delights in the one whose heart is in his gift].

Receive (v)—To take into one's possession (something offered or delivered).

Psalm 27:10 (NIV) - Though my father and mother forsake me, the Lord will receive me.

Resources(n)—A source of supply, support, or aid, especially one that can be readily drawn upon when needed.

1 John 3:17 (AMP)—But whoever has the world's goods (adequate resources), and sees his brother in need, but has no compassion for him, how does the love of God live in him?

Response (n)—An answer or reply, as in words or in some action.

Romans 8:30-31 (NIV)-—30 And those he predestined, he also called; those he called, he also justified; those he justified, he also glorified. 31 What, then, shall we say in response to these things? If God is for us, who can be against us?

Seed (n)—The fertilized, matured ovule of a flowering plant, containing an embryo or rudimentary plant.

Matthew 13:23 (NIV)—But the seed falling on good soil refers to someone who hears the word and understands it. This is the one who produces a crop, yielding a hundred, sixty or thirty times what was sown."

Shine (v)—To give forth or glow with light; shed or cast light.

Psalm 80:3 (NIV)—Restore us, O God; make your face shine on us, that we may be saved.

Surplus (n)(2)—An amount, quantity, etc., greater than needed.

Deuteronomy 28:11 (AMPC)—And the Lord shall make you have a surplus of prosperity, through the fruit of your body, of your livestock, and of your ground, in the land which the Lord swore to your fathers to give you.

Time (n)(19)—The right occasion or opportunity.

Galatians 6:9 (NIV)—Let us not become weary in doing good, for at the proper time we will reap a harvest if we do not give up.

Tithe (n)—The tenth part of agricultural produce or personal income set apart as an offering to God or for works of mercy, or the same amount regarded as an obligation or tax for the support of the church, priesthood, or the like.

Malachi 3:10 (NLT)—Bring all the tithes into the storehouse so there will be enough food in my Temple. "If you do," says the LORD of Heaven's Armies, "I will open the windows of Heaven for you. I will pour out a blessing so great you won't have enough room to take it in! Try it! Put me to the test!"

Treasure (n)(3)—Any thing or person greatly valued or highly prized.

Matthew 6:21 (KJV)—For where your treasure is, there will your heart be also.

Unexpected (adj)—Not expected; unforeseen; surprising.

Proverbs 17:7(TLB)-Truth from a rebel or lies from a king are both unexpected.

REFERENCES

Amplified Bible (AMP). Copyright © 2015 by The Lockman Foundation, La Habra, CA 90631. All rights reserved.

Amplified Bible, Classic Edition (AMPC). Copyright © 1954, 1958, 1962, 1964, 1965, 1987 by The Lockman Foundation.

BibleGateway.com. Accessed July 2022. www.biblegateway.com

BRG Bible (BRG). Blue Red and Gold Letter Edition™ Copyright © 2012 BRG Bible Ministries. Used by Permission. All rights reserved. BRG Bible is a Registered Trademark in U.S. Patent and Trademark Office #4145648

Common English Bible (CEB). Copyright © 2011 by Common English Bible.

Dictionary.com unabridged based on the Random House Unabridged Dictionary©, Random House, Inc. 2021. Accessed July 2022. https://www.dictionary.com

Disciples' Literal New Testament (DLNT). Disciples' Literal New Testament: Serving Modern Disciples by More Fully Reflecting the Writing Style of the Ancient Disciples, Copyright © 2011 Michael J. Magill. All Rights Reserved. Published by Reyma Publishing

Holy Bible, Contemporary English Version (CEV). Copyright © 1995 by American Bible Society.

Holy Bible, King James Version (KJV). Public Domain.

Holy Bible, New International Version®, NIV® (NIV). Copyright © 1973, 1978, 1984, 2011 by Biblica, Inc.® Used by permission. All rights reserved worldwide.

Holy Bible, New King James Version® (NKJV). Copyright © 1982 by Thomas Nelson. Used by permission. All rights reserved.

REFERENCES
(CONTINUED)

Holy Bible, New Living Translation (NLT). Copyright © 1996, 2004, 2015 by Tyndale House Foundation. Used by permission of Tyndale House Publishers, Inc., Carol Stream, Illinois 60188. All rights reserved.

International Children's Bible (ICB). The Holy Bible, International Children's Bible® Copyright© 1986, 1988, 1999, 2015 by Thomas Nelson. Used by permission.

New English Translation (NET). NET Bible® copyright ©1996-2017 by Biblical Studies Press, L.L.C. http://netbible.com All rights reserved.

The Living Bible (TLB). Copyright © 1971 by Tyndale House Foundation. Used by permission of Tyndale House Publishers Inc., Carol Stream, Illinois 60188. All rights reserved.

The Message (MSG). Copyright © 1993, 2002, 2018 by Eugene H. Peterson

The Passion Translation® (TPT). Copyright © 2017, 2018, 2020 by Passion & Fire Ministries, Inc. Used by permission. All rights reserved.

Worldwide English (New Testament) (WE). © 1969, 1971, 1996, 1998 by SOON Educational Publications

BEST-SELLING AUTHORS

From bankruptcy to divorce to remarrying each other and prospering God's way, best-selling authors Angela and Charles Todd figured out (a thing or two...) how to work the word of God to increase and thrive in their finances, marriage, relationships, and health. In 2006, they founded Todd WorldWide Ministries, a 501c3 that helps others succeed spiritually, physically, and financially, and co-host The Abundant Life talk show, sharing their supernatural journey to success (Local Now channel 509 & YouTube). In 2020, while teaching successful ten-week Biblical financial courses, they were awe-struck at their students' breakthroughs, which prompted parents to ask if they could bring their children into class to learn supernatural financial increase principles. 20-20 vision awakened and fueled a passion for teaching kids and families basic money principles that govern increase. So, they found a way to wrap Charles's custom finance curriculum around super fun and engaging animated characters they created called Money Mike & The Gang™.

The main character Money Mike is a super cool animated tree with hidden messages on his money leaves that reveal Biblical secrets to success of how to tithe, save, invest, give, and stay out of debt. The Money Mike & The Gang™ four-book series releasing in 2022/23 includes "Money Is Easy" by Money Mike, "Giving Is Easy" by Giving Grace, "Saving Is Easy" by Saving Sam, and "Say No To Debt" by the bad guy, Loan Shark. The books help kids and families, regardless of what state of money mess they are in, to apply easy steps to break free of debt and poverty to prosper at a very early age. The books also introduce financial vocabulary and include a glossary of definitions and correlating scriptures to help families engage in learning to start having money conversations. The Todds firmly believe it's not the responsibility of children to take care of their parents but that children get set up early in life to prosper so that they can be a blessing to their children's children for generations to follow.

Visit www.toddworldwide.org and www.moneymikeandthegang.com to learn more about the Todds and the books.

MONEY MIKE & THE GANG™

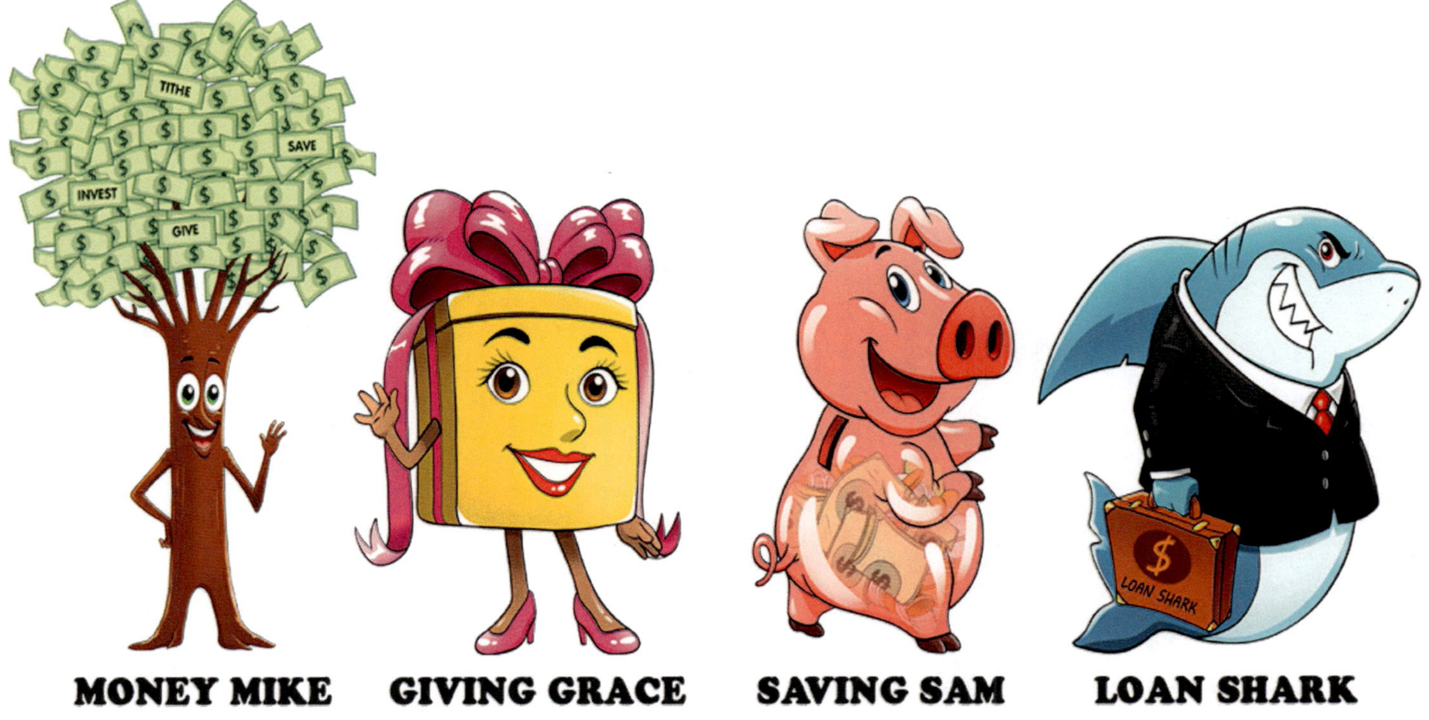

FUN WAYS OF LEARNING HOW TO
TITHE, SAVE, INVEST, GIVE, AND STAY OUT OF DEBT!

WWW.MONEYMIKEANDTHEGANG.COM
@MONEYMIKE_GANG

Made in the USA
Las Vegas, NV
20 August 2023